DON'T DREAD

*Overcoming the
Spirit of Dread
with the Supernatural
Power of God*

⟳ ≈≈≈ ⟲

JOYCE
MEYER

WARNER
Faith®

NEW YORK   BOSTON   NASHVILLE

Unless otherwise indicated, all Scripture quotations are taken from *The Amplified Bible* (AMP). *The Amplified Bible, Old Testament* copyright © 1965, 1987 by The Zondervan Corporation. *The Amplified New Testament,* copyright © 1954, 1958, 1987 by The Lockman Foundation. Used by permission.

Scripture quotations marked (NEB) are taken from *The New English Bible.* © The Delegates of the Oxford University Press and The Syndics of the Cambridge University Press 1961, 1970. Reprinted by permission.

Scripture quotations marked (NKJV) are taken from *The New King James Version.* Copyright © 1979, 1980, 1982, Thomas Nelson, Inc. Used by permission. All rights reserved.

Scriptures marked (KJV) are taken from the *King James Version* of the Bible.

Warner Books Edition
Copyright © 1998 by Joyce Meyer
Life In The Word, Inc.
P.O. Box 655
Fenton, Missouri 63026
All rights reserved.

Warner Faith

Time Warner Book Group
1271 Avenue of the Americas, New York, NY 10020
Visit our Web site at www.twbookmark.com.

Warner Faith® and the Warner Faith logo are trademarks of Time Warner Book Group Inc.

Printed in the United States of America

First Warner Faith Printing: February 2003
10 9 8 7 6 5 4 3

ISBN: 0-446-69172-0
LCCN: 2002115548

CONTENTS

DON'T DREAD

1

THE SILENT DECEPTION

$\mathcal{D}$o you look forward to each day, approaching it with a great expectancy of good things to come? Or do you approach each day in a state of ongoing fear and dread?

God is always calling us up higher into new levels of blessing. He wants us to enjoy life. Jesus came that we might have and enjoy life, and have it in abundance (to the full, till it overflows) according to John 10:10. But dread of ordinary, everyday routine tasks will squeeze the joy and peace right out of life. People dread everything from doing dishes to driving home from work to grocery shopping to doing laundry. They dread getting up in the morning, going to bed in the evening and even dread the entire week!

Dread is a form of fear—just a little flavor of it. Worry is another form of fear. The devil uses fear in forms we don't always recognize to steal our joy and prevent us from living the kind of life God intended.

In the Bible we see God telling people whom He has called to do great things to "fear not" so that fear would not stop them from moving forward according to His will.

The Bible tells us in Second Timothy 1:7 that fear is not from God.

> God did not give us a spirit of timidity (of cowardice, of craven and cringing and fawning fear), but [He has given us a spirit] of power and of love and of

calm and well-balanced mind and
discipline and self-control.

First John 4:18 tells us **fear hath torment**
(KJV). Fear torments and prevents. It prevents us
from walking in the will of God and from moving
forward in the things of God to receive the bless-
ings of God.

We are all aware of fear that is obvious and
recognizable in situations. And when we recognize fear, we know to deal with it. But if we don't
recognize dread of everyday mundane tasks and
little problems as an attack of fear against us, we
won't deal with it. Then the devil will be able to
use that spirit of fear to rob us of enjoying all of
life!

There are probably countless times every
day when we experience different varieties of fear
in our thinking or emotions. Even if we do recognize our situation as being based in fear, many

times we do nothing about it except wish it weren't there.

Often we are afraid of the unknown—of trying new things—and don't even realize we are in fear. When my hairdresser of seven or eight years retired from the hair business, I made an appointment with a new one. As I was driving to the shop, I suddenly realized I was worrying that my hair wouldn't turn out well! I was in fear and almost didn't recognize it!

At that moment the Holy Spirit spoke something to me that changed my life. He said, "Pray about everything and fear nothing."

Pray about Everything
and Fear Nothing

The Bible says, **Be unceasing in prayer [praying perseveringly]** (1 Thessalonians 5:17).

Effective prayer does not depend upon praying in a certain place, at a certain time or in a certain posture. God wants us to be as comfortable praying as we are breathing.

We release faith when we pray, and God wants us to be ready to release our faith at any moment. Then when fear comes knocking on our door, faith will be there to answer—and that's critical! Faith is the only thing that has the strength to overcome fear.

Watch and Pray

The Bible says to watch and pray (Matthew 26:41; Mark 14:38).

> All of you must keep awake (give strict
> attention, be cautious and active) and
> watch and pray, that you may not
> come into temptation. The spirit

indeed is willing, but the flesh is weak
(MATTHEW 26:41).

It is my desire that the Holy Spirit will use
the message in this book to open your eyes to
the importance of recognizing fear in all its forms
so that you will watch for it and be ready to
pray—pray "that you may not come into" the
"temptation" to fear!

Some people think **watch and pray** in the
Bible means to watch everybody else—watch
and judge, watch and criticize! No, it means to
watch *ourselves*. In particular it means to watch
for things that will try to steal from the peace and
joy available to us as children in God's kingdom
(Romans 14:17).

It also means to watch for things that might
try to make us think we are not in rightstanding
with God, or in **righteousness (that state which
makes a person acceptable to God)** (Romans

14:17). If you have received Jesus as your Savior, you are in rightstanding with God (2 Corinthians 5:21). If you did something wrong and asked God for forgiveness, *He has forgiven you!* (1 John 1:9). The minute you begin to feel condemnation, start praying. Don't live in fear that God is displeased with you.

Your Sin Is under the Blood

If the devil starts to bring condemnation on you, talk back with Scriptures. Say, "Now wait a minute . . ."

> *I know what I did was wrong, but I have repented. My sin is under the blood of Jesus Christ.*
>
> *My righteousness is not based upon my doing everything right. I am right with God because He has made me righteous*

through the blood of Jesus. I believe in Jesus Christ, and I am delivered from guilt and condemnation.

My sin is forgiven. The guilt the devil is trying to heap on me has got to go. I am not living under this condemnation any longer. In Jesus' name (based on 1 JOHN 1:7, 9).

As you begin to watch and pray, your eyes will be opened. You will be amazed at how many things you fear or dread. For that reason, the more you talk back with the Scriptures when the devil brings negative feelings and thoughts, the more joy you will experience. Otherwise he will continually beat you over the head with fear, torment, guilt and condemnation to keep you from enjoying life! I let the devil do that to me for years, but I don't let him do it anymore. Still, I continue to be amazed at the things I realize I'm dreading!

I saw this recently when I was getting a facial. Someone gives me facials to be a blessing to me. They are so relaxing, and I feel so good when they are over. The woman who does them has you wear a terry cloth towel as a wrap. I was so comfortable and was enjoying the experience so much, I looked over at the clothes I had worn to the appointment and thought: "I dread putting on all those clothes and going home!"

I didn't want to move on to doing something else that I thought wouldn't be nearly as much fun or as enjoyable as continuing on with the facial. Dread not only took away from my enjoyment of the experience but also destroyed a lingering joy I could have taken with me!

When you are leaving something you enjoyed, the devil has a purpose: to move you right into dreading the next thing so that you will lose the benefit of taking the joy of the experience with you. Note: THE MINUTE WE START DREADING THE NEXT THING, WE STOP ENJOYING THE LAST THING. I see this with people who come to my meetings. At the beginning they are so excited to be there, but as we approach the close of the meeting, they start dreading the drive home.

Do you see how the devil uses dread in almost everything you do to steal your enjoyment of life? If you are like most people, there are only a few times in life when you feel as though you are *really* having a good time. Dread is a spirit of fear sent out from hell to bring destruction!

Power to Defeat Fear

Fear comes after us *aggressively* and *violently*. Because fear is aggressive, we cannot defeat it passively. We must use the power available to us as Christians—aggressive Christianity—against an aggressive devil.

> Little children, you are of God [you
> belong to Him] and have [already]
> defeated and overcome them [the
> agents of the antichrist], because He
> Who lives in you is greater (mightier)
> than he who is in the world (1 JOHN
> 4:4).

The *King James Version* words this verse, **greater is he that is in you, than he that is in the world.** But if we do not draw on the Greater One in us to come against "he that is in the world" then "he that is in the world" will prevail.

Your flesh—the natural, carnal "you"—won't want to confront the devil. It wants to go by feelings. It wants to wish the problem away. It says, "I wish I didn't have to pick up the kids from school"; "I wish I didn't have to go outside, when it's so hot—I don't want to be hot"; "I wish I didn't have to do this"; "I wish I didn't have to do that."

The flesh will keep you defeated and deflated on the inside all the time. Passively letting negative feelings, thoughts—little fears—come on you will put your "wishbone" into operation. Saying things like, "I wish I didn't have these problems with my mind," will not stop the devil from stealing your peace and joy. Aggressively dealing with him will! And we, as believers in Jesus Christ, have the "backbone" to do what it takes to confront him—the Spirit of the living God inside us.

Don't put up with those feelings and thoughts! Use the power of God available to you!

Seize the Kingdom!

And from the days of John the Baptist until the present time, the kingdom of heaven has endured violent assault, and violent men seize it by force [as a precious prize—a share in the heavenly kingdom is sought with most ardent zeal and intense exertion] (MATTHEW 11:12).

We need to become violent Christians, not with people, but with the devil! Be aggressive! Watch yourself—if your peace starts draining out of you, if you start feeling worried or anxious, or if you become judgmental or critical toward people, as soon as you sense or recognize what is happening, aggressively confront the devil— pray! For example, if you realize you are being judgmental or critical of another person, speak out against those thoughts. Say:

I will not be critical or judgmental. The love of God is shed abroad in me by the Holy Ghost according to Romans 5:5, and I will walk in love. I will not walk in judgment and criticism. I will not have a bad attitude toward people. I have problems of my own and, therefore, have no right to judge anyone else. God, forgive me for being critical of that person, and help me now to walk in love. In Jesus' name.

If you have a vague feeling something is wrong and don't know what it is, ask God, "What is going on here?" He will show you.

You may realize the problem is worry, or that you did something wrong and have not repented, or that you mistreated someone then acted as if it didn't matter.

God will show you why you do not have peace or joy. So many times if I felt something was wrong but couldn't identify it and asked the

Lord, "What is the matter?" He has answered, "Fear." And, sure enough, I realized I was fearing something.

You will be amazed at how quickly you are delivered from those hidden attacks of the devil as you watch and pray!

"No Fear in Love"

First John 4:18, KJV, says, **There is no fear in love.** The *Amplified Version* says:

> There is no fear in love [*dread does not exist*], but full-grown (complete, perfect) love turns fear out of doors and expels every trace of terror!

You may know God loves you, but still have fear. If so, you need to continue growing in your understanding of God's love for you because when you know *how much* God loves you, fear disappears: **dread does not exist!**

God loves you and wants to bless you more than you can possibly imagine. He wants to give you victory in every area: over sin, in your health and finances, socially, and He wants to give you joy. He wants you to receive His love moment by moment in every situation by walking in faith and trusting Him for everything.

Perfect love casteth out fear (1 John 4:18 KJV), and God is that perfect love. Once you have a revelation of how perfect that love is toward you, nothing will cause you to fear.

2

~~~~~~

ANOINTED TO DO THE ORDINARY

*H*ebrews 12:1 through 3 says to run the race with endurance, looking to Jesus so that you may not grow weary or exhausted, losing heart and relaxing and fainting in your minds (v. 3).

Do you look at a sink full of dirty dishes and want to faint in your mind? Does the thought of mowing the lawn get you depressed? Do you dread making a particular phone call or even a party you are planning?

God has taught me that to enjoy life, I must learn how to enjoy *every*thing.

You may ask, "Now, how could I enjoy cleaning house?" It all depends on your mindset.

Dread Is a Mindset

The devil has programmed us with a mindset to enjoy certain things but to dread others.

For example my daughter said to me, "I remember when I dreaded working all week, but I really looked forward to the weekends. As soon as the weekends came near the end, I started dreading going to work again."

There is no telling how many millions of people dread their jobs. But if you are working, you might as well enjoy it. Dread will steal any joy you could experience when working, and it will also steal your joy while you are away from work as you are dreading going back!

As Christians, we can do unpleasant things and enjoy them because the Holy Spirit is in us.

We can enjoy Him in the midst of adverse or unpleasant conditions. This is a privilege that unsaved people do not have. Our joy comes from Who is *inside* us.

Reset Your Mindset

Last year my husband, Dave, and I and some of our ministry team went to India. The flight lasted around sixteen hours—a lot of hours to sit on a plane!

If you have a mindset of dread, you will have a mouthful of dread. I found myself saying, "I am dreading being on a plane for sixteen hours. Sitting still that long is really hard for me, and I know that trip will be boring!" I could have said, "I'm looking forward to going to India—I believe God will make the trip interesting. We are going to have a great time on that plane."

God began to show us that if we set our minds on enjoying the trip, it wouldn't be bad. We set our minds to enjoy each other and for the time to go by quickly. And we enjoyed the trip!

As believers in Jesus, we are supernatural people. We can decide ahead of time to enjoy doing something we would not normally consider enjoyable. We can set ourselves up for joy or for misery. It all depends on the attitude we decide to have.

When we are dreading something, we can make a decision and state: "I am *not* going to dread that." Then we can release our faith through praying by simply saying, "Lord, I thank You that You are helping me perform this task. It is unpleasant in the natural realm, but Your anointing can come on me to make this pleasant. Because I am supernatural, I can enjoy this task even though other people might not. The devil is not going to steal my joy in this, in Jesus' name."

If we dread cleaning house but have to clean it anyway, what is the sense in dreading it? Instead we might approach it this way: "I have the house to clean, and I will do it with a good attitude. I have the joy of the Lord. I can enjoy anything. *Anything!*"

If we set our minds to it, we can enjoy everything we do in life.

Being "Spiritual"

Several years ago God began revealing something to me: I saw spiritual things as being very important and I enjoyed them, but I dreaded all the "secular" tasks in life. I felt they were things that I should hurry and get finished so I could get back to doing something spiritual. The devil was using that deception as another way to rob my joy.

I used to feel really good about myself, happy about myself, when I was praying or reading the Word, listening to praise music or a teaching tape, or when I was in a spiritual meeting doing things I felt were important. I felt good about "spiritual" things I did because I thought those things were pleasing to God.

I wanted to finish natural, "secular," tasks such as grocery shopping and housecleaning as quickly as possible so that I could go back to doing the things I thought were really important.

The bottom line is, we spend more time doing those mundane, routine tasks than we spend doing anything else. God wants to anoint us in a supernatural way to handle ordinary, everyday tasks, so that we can be exceedingly joyful in the midst of them. This is the area where we can be witnesses to the world.

Anybody can enjoy life when having a good time. But Christians can enjoy life no matter what the circumstances because we know that God is always looking for ways to reveal His love to us in every moment. Remember, God's love casts out fear, and dread is fear. Therefore when we dread things, we are not walking in the reality of God's love and care for us. Refuse to dread and start enjoying *every* aspect of your life.

3

∽✦∽

FAITHFUL
IN THE LITTLE THINGS

We have in us the same power as Almighty God Who raised Jesus from the dead! (Romans 8:11). If a sink full of dirty dishes defeats us and the thought of going to the grocery store makes us faint, this is a pretty good indicator that we are not using the power that is ours through Christ. If something like getting dressed after a facial and driving home puts us in dread, we are not really enjoying life.

Drawing on God's power to enjoy doing the little ordinary things that take up most of our time usually doesn't even occur to us. But if these ordinary tasks are a continual problem for us, it should be pretty obvious that the devil is using dread as a major attack on the body of Christ. If this silent deceiver can cause us to dread the routine, mundane tasks, he can keep us from walking victoriously in all areas of our lives. Dreading all those little things—things that we think don't really matter—is what steals our joy.

Through the parable in Matthew 25:21, God tells us if we are faithful over a few things, He will make us ruler over many things. People in my meetings laugh when I make the following statement, but it gets my point across: If you don't have authority over a sink full of dirty dishes, there's not much point in trying to cast the devil out of someone!

We think we are supposed to use God's power only on all the big "spiritual" things. We want to use it to rebuke the devil, or reach new levels of prosperity or to bring other great breakthroughs and success.

Yes, God did give us His power for all the big "spiritual" things—for ourselves and to minister supernaturally to others. But a major reason God gave us His power is to enable us to live victoriously moment by moment every day. He wants us to handle the ordinary, routine tasks of our lives without being defeated by our feelings and thoughts as are unbelievers. Joy should be ours on a regular basis.

God gave us a spiritual inheritance to enjoy.

In Him we also were made [God's]
heritage (portion) and we obtained
an inheritance; for we had been
foreordained (chosen and appointed
beforehand) in accordance with His
purpose, Who works out everything

in agreement with the counsel and
design of His [own] will,

So that we who first hoped in
Christ [who first put our confidence
in Him have been destined and
appointed to] live for the praise of His
glory! (EPHESIANS 1:11, 12).

We can use our spiritual inheritance to
live with a sense of peace and security that comes
from knowing who we are and Whose we are.

Watch and pray. Watch for fear, dread, torment, anxiety and worry in your life and say:
"No! I'm not living like this! God has allotted
peace and joy for me! I'm going to work hard to
spend every bit of the inheritance He gave me.
When I go to heaven and see Him face-to-face, I
want to be sure I have spent everything He gave
me to use on earth!"

Confront Problems When They Are Small

One thing most people do not enjoy is confrontation with other people. They dread it!

A large number of people now work on the staff of our ministry, Life In The Word. They are wonderful people, whom I appreciate very much, but of course, they are not perfect. It seems we are always dealing with a personnel situation that requires correction.

I used to dread correcting staff members. Some people don't take correction very well. I don't want to hurt people's feelings or make them mad. But to have a powerful ministry free from strife, I have no choice but to confront the issues that arise.

Several years ago God gave me a revelation that strife is a spirit sent from hell to destroy. It brings destruction to marriages, churches, businesses—relationships. He showed me we had to keep it out of our lives.

A lack of confrontation opens the door to strife. Sometimes when you see a small problem brewing, you may not deal with it for the very reason it is so small. You just would rather not bother with it, or you think it might go away on its own. However, if you do not confront a problem when it is small, it will not go away—it will only get bigger. And bigger!

The Little Foxes

. . . Take for us the foxes, the little foxes that spoil the vineyards [of our love], for our vineyards are in blossom (SONG OF SOLOMON 2:15).

So often we think our lives will be fine if we can solve the big problems. But frequently the little problems, "the little foxes," are the ones that keep us down.

If someone says or does something to you that causes offense and you do not deal with it, you will have a tiny problem. The next time that person hurts your feelings, you will have another tiny problems. Every time the person hurts your feelings, your tiny problem gets a little bigger. Then at some point when that person does something inconsequential, without previous warning, you will just blow up!

Why? Because you didn't deal with the little problems as they came along. When you first see a little problem, confront it on the spot. Pray. Speak out loud to it if you are someplace where you can.

If someone offends you, immediately say: *Lord, I forgive that person. I refuse offense. I will not store up this offense because I refuse to live in torment. I will not let the devil steal my joy, in Jesus' name.*

If you start dealing with all the little things you are dreading, dealing with the big things will come easily!

When I was first learning how to believe God for finances, it was more fearful for me to believe God for my kids' tennis shoes than it is now to believe God for the millions of dollars I need to run this ministry. Why? Because my faith developed on the little things.

Many people do not want to take time to handle little things. Then when the major problems come along, they are unprepared and can't handle them.

Aggressively attacking small problems and tasks will bring you joy, if not right away, eventually:

Thou hast been faithful over a few
things, I will make thee ruler over

many things: enter thou into the joy of thy lord (MATTHEW 25:21 KJV).

Make a decision that you are going to deal with every issue God shows you to confront no matter how small or large. Don't dread confronting the issues; instead, know that God will help you do everything He leads you to do. He will give us the wisdom and courage we need if we are willing to step out.

4

GOD HAS GIVEN YOU THE LAND—POSSESS IT!

Remember, it will take aggressive Christianity to confront those dreads and seize our inheritance in God's kingdom.

God called the Israelites out of bondage in Egypt to go to the land He had promised to give them as a perpetual inheritance—a land flowing with milk and honey (Leviticus 20:24), a land of prosperity. God had already given the Israelites the Promised Land. They just needed to go in and possess it!

Behold, the Lord your God has set the
land before you; go up and possess it,
as the Lord, the God of your fathers,
has said to you. Fear not, neither be
dismayed (DEUTERONOMY 1:21).

Ten of the twelve people Moses sent ahead
to spy out the land brought back a bad report—
even though the land was good, giants were
there! Immediately, the Israelites began to faint
in their minds—they wept all night (Numbers
13:33; 14:1; Deuteronomy 1:21–25).

Deuteronomy 1:25 through 30 gives the
account:

And they took of the fruit of the land
in their hands and brought it down to
us and brought us word again, and
said, It is a good land which the Lord
our God gives us.

Yet you would not go up, but rebelled against the commandment of the Lord your God.

You were peevish and discontented in your tents, and said,

Because the Lord hated us, He brought us forth out of the land of Egypt to deliver us into the hand of the Amorites to destroy us.

To what are we going up? Our brethren have made our hearts melt, saying, The people are bigger and taller than we are; the cities are great and fortified to the heavens. And moreover we have seen the [giantlike] sons of the Anakim there.

Then I said to you, Dread not, neither be afraid of them.

The Lord your God Who goes before you, He will fight for you just

as He did for you in Egypt before your
eyes.

The Israelites saw that the Lord had given
them a good land. He told them to go in and
possess it—not to fear, be dismayed or dread.
But instead, the Israelites decided not to trust
Him. They became **peevish and discontented in
their tents.** They thought the Lord hated them
because He was leading them into a confrontation. They gave in to their fears and rebelled
against His command to take the land.

Their mouths were full of dread. By saying
they would be handed over to the Amorites, the
Israelites prophesied their own doom. Before
fighting the battle, they had already decided they
had lost.

Because we believers are **temples of the
Holy Ghost** (1 Corinthians 6:19 kjv), I believe
our flesh is now the "tent" of the Lord. Some-

times we get that peevish discontented attitude in our flesh. If we end up in a situation which seems as bad as one God just brought us out of, we blame Him and say, "If You loved me, You would deliver me from this situation. You must hate me or you would never have brought me out here to face this enemy. This is too hard!" We give in to our fears instead of confronting them.

Anointed to Go Through

In difficult situations like the ones above, God is anointing us to *face, confront* and go *through* them. He is anointing us to aggressively possess the land—to seize the kingdom by force! Yes, He does deliver us from some situations, but in others He anoints us to go *through*. Psalm 23:4 KJV says, **Yea, though I walk through the valley of the shadow of death, I will fear no evil.**

The devil tells us something is "too hard" to

try to get us to give up. Deuteronomy 30:11 tells us, **For this commandment which I command you this day is not too difficult for you, nor is it far off.** The Lord's commandments are not too difficult for those who believe in Him because His Spirit is inside us to work powerfully on our behalf to help us do what He asks.

Isaiah 8:11, 12 (NEB) tells us that believers are not to fear what others fear: **These were the words of the Lord to me . . . you shall neither dread nor fear that which they fear.** The things the world fears are not our inheritance.

You are the only one who controls your attitude. You can fear and dread what the world fears, or you can put your trust in God and believe He will do what He says in His Word.

Where God Guides, He Provides

With God's power inside us, we should be able to handle anything coming against us. No wonder the apostle Paul said, **I can do all things through Christ which strengtheneth me** (Philippians 4:13 KJV). The *Amplified Bible* says, . . . [I am ready for anything and equal to anything through Him Who infuses inner strength into me; I am self-sufficient in Christ's sufficiency].

If we look at all the things we need to do in the future, we often feel overwhelmed and begin to dread them. But where God guides, He provides. We can trust Him to give us the grace (the power of the Holy Spirit) to do things when the time comes to do them. God rarely gives us what we need until we need it. He gave the Israelites manna one day at a time. If they tried to gather the next day's portion, it rotted and stank

(Exodus 16:20). We can rest in the knowledge of God's provision for us and trust Him.

Develop a mindset that says, "I'm ready for anything; I'm equal to anything." Determine in your heart to possess the land the Lord has given you. As a born-again believer, you are anointed to walk through. You can be free from being timid, faint-hearted, fearful and full of dread. Just begin confronting the devil. Stop letting what he is offering push you down. Rise up against it!

Say to that sink full of dirty dishes, "You are not defeating me, in Jesus' name! An hour from now you are going to be washed, dried and put away. And the whole time I am working, I'm going to sing and be happy!"

God has already given us the Promised Land. Our part is to confront those dreads and possess it!

5

~~~

ENJOY LIFE ANYWAY

*I*f we are experiencing a repetitive problem, we may think we cannot enjoy life as long as we have that problem. This is another mindset the devil tries to program into us to steal our joy. God wants us to have victory in every area and enjoy life no matter what the circumstances. He has provided victory and joy for us—we just need to go in and possess the land!

If the devil has programmed you with a mindset, you can change it. Colossians 3:2 tells us to keep our minds set on things above.

If then you have been raised with Christ [to a new life, thus sharing His resurrection from the dead], aim at and seek the [rich, eternal treasures] that are above, where Christ is, seated at the right hand of God.

And *set your minds and keep them set on what is above* (the higher things), not on the things that are on the earth.

For [as far as this world is concerned] you have died, and your [new, real] life is hidden with Christ in God (COLOSSIANS 3:1–3).

The Lord showed my husband, Dave, how to change his mindset and enjoy life while dealing with a repetitive problem. Dave had migraine headaches regularly for years from the time he was a young boy.

If you have never had a true migraine headache, it is difficult to imagine the pain. A migraine headache can make you sick to your stomach. Dave had the kind so severe, he saw light flashes before his eyes. Even though the headaches were bad, the way he felt afterward bothered him more. Sometimes after the headache is gone, the person will feel funny for a period of time—slightly detached, or unable to fully participate in what is happening around him.

Dave dreaded those headaches—he had developed a mindset that he could not enjoy life while he was experiencing them. But God began to show him not to dread them. The Lord impressed upon Dave, "You need to get a new mindset of 'I'm not dreading these' . . ." and told him, "Don't be impressed by the problem."

Be Impressed by God's Word

Be impressed by God's *power*. In essence God was saying to Dave, "Believe that my power is enough to cause you to be able to go ahead and enjoy your life even in the midst of these headaches."

Any of us who live with various aches and pains in our body while waiting for healing to manifest have two choices: we can let the problem make our life totally miserable, or we can choose to make the best out of life in the meantime. Those of us who make the decision to go on will enjoy life much more than those who decide to do nothing but "baby-sit" the problem by thinking and talking about it.

Dave made a decision to believe God's power would enable him to make the best of life in the midst of the ongoing problem.

People who experience migraine headaches can feel them starting before they reach full force. The next time Dave started to get one of those headaches, he confronted it immediately and said, "I'm not afraid of you. I'm not impressed by you. I'm not going to dread you. I've made a decision—I'm enjoying my life anyway."

After Dave changed his mindset to believe God would supernaturally enable him to enjoy life in spite of the headaches, do you know what happened? He was delivered from them. They disappeared!

Aggressively Confront Every *Attack of the Devil*

Dave confronted the headache just as soon as he felt it start. God wants to deliver us from fear and dread by bringing us to a point of taking a confrontational attitude against any attack the devil uses to try to destroy us or steal our joy.

Sometimes when we first start getting physical symptoms in our body, we almost wait to see how sick we will become before praying against them. As we saw before in dealing with people, when we first see a problem, we need to confront it on the spot; otherwise, it *will* get bigger! First Peter 5:9 says, **Withstand him** [the devil—v. 8]; **be firm in faith** [against his onset . . .]. Watch and pray to recognize any attack of the devil and confront him at the onset!

You will be amazed how much trouble you will avoid by resisting the devil at the first sign of an attack. As soon as the symptoms start to come on you, confront them aggressively by praying in the name of Jesus for His healing power to touch you. Lay hands on yourself, or ask someone to agree with you in prayer.

If Dave and I get up in the morning and he says, "I don't feel very good," or I say, "I've got a headache," we pray immediately.

At one of my meetings my aunt came to me at the tape table and said, "Pray for me; I'm starting to lose my voice." She had dealt with pneumonia several times because of some problems with her lungs. Losing her voice had been the first sign she was getting pneumonia. I laid hands on her and prayed. She told me later that before she reached home, her voice had come back completely.

She could have waited, thinking, something like, "I wonder if I'm getting sick; no, it's probably just the altitude—there's nothing I can do about it." Instead she immediately confronted the symptoms by asking for prayer.

The devil gives us a whole bagful of excuses to get us to accept his nonsense! He doesn't want us to stop his attacks by confronting him with the power of the Living God inside us!

A New Mindset

If you think you cannot enjoy life because of a repetitive problem—a certain person you deal with regularly or an unpleasant task you often need to do—you can choose to make the best out of life in spite of the problem.

Wherever we set our minds, our emotions follow. For example, if you hear the name of someone you have not thought about in a long time who hurt your feelings, you may start thinking about the person and the incident and become upset. The longer you think, the more upset you become, then suddenly, you are dealing with anger. You can change from being totally calm to emotionally violent because of what you choose to think about and dwell on. Instead of thinking about the ongoing problem, you can set your mind in a different direction.

Dave had that problem of migraine head-aches as part of his life from childhood, week after week, month after month, and he was delivered in a moment after he changed his mind-set! It has been years and years since then, and in all that time migraine headaches have tried to come on him probably three times. The first time Dave started to get one was after he testified at one of our meetings about being delivered from them! Within a day or two, after not having had one in years, he started getting one of those headaches!

Do you see what is happening here? There are spirits behind these problems! So many of the problems afflicting us are spirits coming out of hell to attack and try to destroy us! They are from the enemy and we must boldly confront him.

The devil uses these ongoing problems to squeeze the joy out of our lives by getting us in a pattern of dread. Whether the problem is a headache, backache or symptoms some women experience during their cycle each month, the minute we feel one tiny indication of a symptom, we start to dread. "Oh no, here it comes."

How can we enjoy life when we are so in bondage to dread, we dread the dread?

First John 3:8 tells us, . . . the reason the Son of God was made manifest (visible) was to undo (destroy, loosen, and dissolve) the works the devil [has done].

James 4:7 says, . . . Resist the devil [stand firm against him], and he will flee from you.

First Peter 5:8 says, . . . that enemy of yours, the devil, roams around like a lion roaring. . . . It does not say he is one; it says he is like one.

Smith Wigglesworth told the story of seeing a pet dog follow a lady out of her house and run all around her feet. "She said to the dog, 'My dear, I cannot have you with me today.' The dog wagged its tail and made a big fuss. She said, 'Go home, my dear.' But the dog did not go. At last she shouted roughly, 'Go home,' and off it went. Some people deal with the devil like that. The devil can stand all the comfort you like to give him. Cast him out!"[1]

The devil and all the demons he sends out after us are like that dog. When we say, "Go!" resisting him in the power of God, he will flee!

The enemy will be revealed one day, and if we have lived our life in fear, we will look at him and say, "You're the one I cowered from all my life? You're the one who deceived the nations? You?"

The devil goes about *like* a roaring lion, but we *have* the Lion of Judah (Hosea 5:14) inside

1. Roberts Liardon, comp., SMITH WIGGLESWORTH: *The Complete Collection of His Life Teachings,* (Tulsa: Albury Publishing, 1996), p. 346.

us! God has given us the power to make the devil flee! Be determined.

Some of us have longstanding problems that developed before we knew anything about dealing with them spiritually. But, thank God, we can start the process of reversal and confront the new attacks of the enemy at the same time we are dealing with some of the older problems that have already grown roots. The ones with roots are harder to get rid of, but it can be done.

In the natural realm, it would have been impossible for Dave to recover as he did from the headaches he had experienced for years. And even though the longstanding problem had very deep roots, the headaches disappeared instantly!

Sometimes the manifestation is instant, and sometimes it is the result of a process. But in either case at the first sign of the devil, resist him. **And he will flee from you!**

6

Faith Has an Attitude

To enjoy *all* the inheritance God has for you, get in agreement with Him to receive *all* He wants to give you. Amos 3:3 (kjv) says, **Can two walk together, except they be agreed?** Get in agreement with God to set your mind and keep it set in the right direction.

Joyful Expectancy of Good

If we have the right attitude of faith, God's power will come on us to make the hard things we need to do pleasant, enjoyable and fun. A Holy Spirit ease will come on us. But if we do things with a bad attitude, we will only be miserable.

As we saw before in Deuteronomy 1:27, the Israelites had a bad attitude! They **were peevish and discontented** [they **murmured**, KJV; they **complained**, NKJV] **in** their **tents**. They thought possessing the land would be too hard if not impossible. They did not want to confront the situation. They wanted everything to come to them easily.

In spite of the miracles the Lord had done for them in delivering and leading them, the Israelites did not trust Him to guide, protect and enable them to take the land (Verses 30–32). They trusted their fears instead!

> It is [only] eleven days' journey from
> Horeb by the way of Mount Seir to
> Kadesh-barnea [on Canaan's border;

yet Israel took forty years to get beyond it] (DEUTERONOMY 1:2).

The Israelites' trip to the Promised Land which could have been completed in eleven days took forty years because of their complaining and unbelief! (See Numbers 14:26–35; Deuteronomy 1:26–40.) Complaining opens the door for the enemy to come in and destroy. (See 1 Corinthians 10:10.)

Faith's attitude is one of leaning on God, trusting and being confident in Him—it is a joyful expectancy of good. Rather than dreading something by anticipating that it will make us miserable, we can have faith God will give us the power to enjoy it.

I made my mind up a few years ago I was not going to live in any more misery. I said, "God, I'm missing something here—I'm doing all the spiritual things everybody tells me to do, and I'm still miserable."

Much of the answer was in applying the principles the Lord showed me that I have included in this book to a lot of simple, practical things. The gospel is practical! Some of the problems we think are so overwhelming are not nearly as bad as the problem caused by allowing dread and fear to steal our joy in many little ways. We spend the majority of our time handling the things *outside* us when we should concentrate on allowing God to deal with the things going on *inside* us.

Our joy, peace, righteousness and power are on the *inside* of us. Romans 8:11 tells us the same Spirit that raised Christ from the dead lives *inside* us and shall quicken our mortal body.

The quickening power of God can come on everything we do. It is like lightning! God's power can fall on us and energize us to do mundane, ordinary, everyday tasks with great joy. Ephesians 5:18 tells us, . . . **do not get drunk with wine** . . . **but ever be filled and stimulated with the [Holy] Spirit.**

When we approach life by maintaining an inner attitude of setting our minds on **the higher things**, we will not even notice the enemy's attempts to attack us with little dreads and fears as we go about our work or do other things. If we stay full of the right thing by setting our thoughts on Who God is and the spiritual inheritance made available to us through Jesus, the wrong thing, Satan's attempts to steal our joy through deceiving thoughts, will have no place in us. Good overcomes evil (Romans 12:21), but we must choose the good.

We can keep our minds on the higher things by applying Ephesians 5:18 -20.

Speak out to one another in psalms
and hymns and spiritual songs, offering
praise with voices [and instruments]
and making melody with all your heart
to the Lord,

At all times and for everything
giving thanks in the name of our Lord
Jesus Christ to God the Father (VERSES
19, 20).

Again, Colossians 3:2, 3 says:

And set your minds and keep them set
on what is above (the higher things),
not on the things that are on the
earth. *For [as far as this world is
concerned] you have died,* and your
[new, real] life is hidden with Christ in
God.

We are able to set our minds on the higher things because we have died to the evil desires of the world described in Colossians 3:4, 5. Those evil desires include fear and dread. Think power thoughts, not fear and dread thoughts.

> When Christ, Who is our life, appears, then you also will appear with Him in [the splendor of His] glory.
>
> So kill (deaden, deprive of power) the evil desire lurking in your members [those animal impulses and all that is earthly in you that is employed in sin]: sexual vice, impurity, sensual appetites, unholy desires, and all greed and covetousness, for that is idolatry (the deifying of self and other created things instead of God).

Faith Is in the Now

Faith is always now. Most of us spend a great deal of time thinking about yesterday and tomorrow living in what I call the regrets and dreads. We regret something we did. We cannot do anything about it now except ask God to cover it so that we can get some good out of it some way, some how. Romans 8:28 (KJV) says: **And we know that all things work together for good to them that love God, to them who are the called according to his purpose.**

Of course, we don't want to get carried away and have a flippant attitude about sin! But you can spend your life regretting all the mistakes you have made. You can regret your marriage failed or that you failed at a job or missed an opportunity and don't see any way of recouping. "God, I'm sorry I did this"; "I regret I did that"; "I wish I hadn't done that." But you must come to a point of receiving forgiveness and go on.

If you live in those regrets, you are not living in faith because faith is now. Faith is for *right* now, *today*. My faith today says my past can be taken care of. *Right now* if I have that joyful expectancy of good, my faith *today* can say, "God can do something about my past and cause all that has happened to even work for my good." Then if I believe *today* that God can take care of my past, *today* I can have joy.

If, because of my mindset and emotions, I'm playing around with yesterday, thinking and worrying about things I cannot do anything about, I'm wasting today. If I'm trying to figure out everything about the future and dreading upcoming events, I'm losing today.

Set Your Mind for Victory

When you get up in the morning, begin the day with an attitude of faith. Set your mind for victory. Think about what you have to do, then set your mind to do it with exuberance and joy, and without dread, fear, murmuring, grumbling or complaining.

An attitude of dread says, "I cannot enjoy my life while doing some of the things I need to do today. I really wish I didn't have to do them."

An attitude of faith says:

When Christ died on the cross, I died with Him. I am legally and positionally dead to evil desires including fear and dread. Fear does not come from God. I don't have to live under fear, so I consider myself dead to those things. I am dead to living in fear.

Fear and dread will not come and have a relationship with me today because I have the same Spirit

64

that raised Christ from the dead living inside me to fight them. I am not going to accept what the devil is trying to put on me. I will not regret the past and dread the future; I will not fear.

I put my trust and confidence in God and joyfully expect good to happen today, because Jesus came that I might have and enjoy life in abundance. In Jesus' name.

God worked and worked with me to keep me living in the now. I made a decision not to lose *today* any more. I'm going to live and enjoy today and enjoy my entire life. What about you?

7

SCRIPTURES TO COMBAT DREAD

As we have seen in many Scriptures, the Lord tells us to neither dread nor fear. The Lord also assures us that we are able to do this! His commands are not difficult (Deuteronomy 30:11,14), and He gives us the ability to do them. (Philippians 4:13.)

> . . . Keep awake (give strict attention, be cautious and active) and watch and pray, that you may not come into temptation. The spirit indeed is

willing, but the flesh is weak.

MATTHEW 26:41

Be earnest and unwearied and steadfast in your prayer [life], being [both] alert and intent in [your praying] with thanksgiving.

COLOSSIANS 4:2

For this reason we also, from the day we heard of it, have not ceased to pray and make [special] request for you, [asking] that you may be filled with the full (deep and clear) knowledge of His will in all spiritual wisdom [in comprehensive insight into the ways and purposes of God] and in understanding and discernment of spiritual things.

COLOSSIANS 1:9

. . . Be strong, vigorous, and very courageous. Be not afraid, neither be dismayed, for the Lord your God is with you wherever you go.

JOSHUA 1:9

The Lord of hosts—regard Him as holy and honor His holy name [by regarding Him as your only hope of safety], and let Him be your fear and let Him be your dread [lest you offend Him by your fear of man and distrust of Him].

ISAIAH 8:13

His master said to him, Well done, you upright (honorable, admirable) and faithful servant! You have been faithful and trustworthy over a little; I will put you in charge of much. Enter into and share the joy (the delight, the blessedness) which your master enjoys.

MATTHEW 25:21

For God did not give us a spirit of
timidity (of cowardice, of craven and
cringing and fawning fear), but [He
has given us a spirit] of power and of
love and of calm and well-balanced
mind and discipline and self-control.

2 TIMOTHY 1:7

There is no fear in love [dread does
not exist], but full-grown (complete,
perfect) love turns fear out of doors
and expels every trace of terror!

1 JOHN 4:18

Behold, the Lord your God has set the
land before you; go up and possess it,
as the Lord, the God of your fathers,
has said to you. Fear not, neither be
dismayed.

DEUTERONOMY 1:21

I have strength for all things in Christ
Who empowers me [I am ready for
anything and equal to anything
through Him Who infuses inner
strength into me; I am self-sufficient
in Christ's sufficiency].

PHILIPPIANS 4:13

Yes, though I walk through the [deep,
sunless] valley of the shadow of death,
I will fear or dread no evil, for You are
with me. . . .

PSALM 23:4

If then you have been raised with
Christ [to a new life, thus sharing His
resurrection from the dead], aim at
and seek the [rich, eternal treasures]
that are above, where Christ is, seated
at the right hand of God.

And set your minds and keep them set
on what is above (the higher things),

71

not on the things that are on the
earth.

For [as far as this world is concerned]
you have died, and your [new, real]
life is hidden with Christ in God.

COLOSSIANS 3:1–3

. . . whatever is true, whatever is
worthy of reverence and is honorable
and seemly, whatever is just, whatever
is pure, whatever is lovely and lovable,
whatever is kind and winsome and
gracious, if there is any virtue and
excellence, if there is anything worthy
of praise, think on and weigh and take
account of these things [fix your
minds on them].

PHILIPPIANS 4:8

Watch for those little fears and dreads that
come to destroy your enjoyment of life. Ask God

to help you recognize them, then confront them with His Word. Replace a mindset of dread with a mindset of "dread is dead, and faith is alive!" Learn to live victoriously moment by moment every day, and experience the joy of living a victorious life.

ABOUT THE AUTHOR

JOYCE MEYER has been teaching the Word of God since 1976 and in full-time ministry since 1980. She is the bestselling author of more than fifty inspirational books, including *How to Hear from God, Knowing God Intimately*, and *Battlefield of the Mind*. She has also released thousands of teaching cassettes and a complete video library. Joyce's *Enjoying Everyday Life* radio and television programs are broadcast around the world, and she travels extensively conducting conferences. Joyce and her husband, Dave, are the parents of four grown children and make their home in St. Louis, Missouri.

To contact the author write:

Joyce Meyer Ministries
P. O. Box 655
Fenton, Missouri 63026
or call: (636) 349-0303

Internet Address: www.joycemeyer.org

Please include your testimony or help received from this book when you write. Your prayer requests are welcome.

To contact the author
in Canada, please write:
Joyce Meyer Ministries Canada, Inc.
Lambeth Box 1300
London, ON N6P 1T5
or call: (636) 349-0303

In Australia, please write:
Joyce Meyer Ministries—Australia
Locked Bag 77
Mansfield Delivery Centre
Queensland 4122
or call: (07) 3349 1200

In England, please write:
Joyce Meyer Ministries
P. O. Box 1549
Windsor
SL4 1GT
or call: (0) 1753 831102

JOYCE MEYER TITLES

Me and My Big Mouth!
Me and My Big Mouth! Study Guide
Prepare to Prosper
Do It Afraid!
Expect a Move of God in Your Life…Suddenly!
Enjoying Where You Are on the Way to Where You Are Going
The Most Important Decision You Will Ever Make
When, God, When?
Why, God, Why?
The Word, the Name, the Blood
Battlefield of the Mind
Battlefield of the Mind Study Guide
Tell Them I Love Them
Peace
The Root of Rejection
If Not for the Grace of God
If Not for the Grace of God Study Guide

JOYCE MEYER SPANISH TITLES
Las Siete Cosas Que Te Roban el Gozo
(Seven Things That Steal Your Joy)
Empezando Tu Día Bien (Starting Your Day Right)

BY DAVE MEYER
Life Lines